An Introduction to Internet of Things, Artificial Intelligence, and Machine Learning

Table of Contents

1. Internet of Things

As technologies develop and grow more complex by the day, the world around us grows more interconnected and intelligent. What once was only fiction, a figment of our imagination has already become part of our reality today. In this document, we hope you will learn something about some of the most integral technologies of our age: The Internet of Things, Artificial Intelligence, and Machine Learning.

1.1 Introduction to the Internet of Things

Let us begin with The Internet of Things! The Internet of things (IoT), essentially, is a network of physical objects, or "things", that have been equipped with sensors, software, and other technologies for the purpose of connecting, communicating and exchanging data with various other similarly connected devices and systems with the help of the Internet.

The size of the devices connected to the Internet of Things can range from anything as small as tiny chips or tags, a recent example being that of the Apple Tag, to large appliances, such as a smart fridge, home security systems, cars, or various industrial machines used in a large variety of sectors. By the end of 2018, there were an estimated 22 billion internet of things (IoT) connected devices in use around the world. As the complexity of both hardware and software in the consumer electronics industry increases dramatically, more and more electronic devices manufactured around the world are produced to have internet connectivity inherent in them. Forecasts suggest that by 2030 around 50 billion of these IoT devices will be in use around the world, creating a massive web of interconnected devices that someone living in the modern world will encounter from the comfort of their home to their workplace.

The value of the Internet of things has only grown in the past years. In a recent study by Fortune Business Insights™ titled, "Internet of Things (IoT) Market Size, Share & Covid-19 Impact Analysis, By Component (Platform, Solution and Services), By Platform (Device Management, Cloud Platform, and Network Management), By Solution (Real-Time Streaming Analytics, Security, Data Management, Remote Monitoring, Network Band Management), By End-Use (BFSI, Retail, Government, Healthcare, Manufacturing, Transportation, IT & Telecom, and Others), and Regional Forecast, 2020-2027.", it is reported that the Internet of Things (IoT) market size had reached USD 250.72 billion in 2019 and is projected to reach USD 1,463.19 billion by 2027, with a Compound Annual Growth Rate of 24.9% during the forecast period. If there is one thing for certain, it is that IoT will be here to stay.

1.2 How the Internet of Things came to be

The main idea of a network of smart devices emerged as early as 1982, beginning with a modified Coca-Cola vending machine at Carnegie Mellon University, which was the first machine connected to the Internet. It was able to send information via the Internet about its inventory as well as if its stock was cold or not.

In 1991, Mark Weiser published a paper, "The Computer of the 21st Century", on ubiquitous computing (a concept in software engineering and computer science that looks at computing occurring anywhere, using any device or machine, and in any format.). This, combined with academic venues such as PerCom and UbiCom gave rise to the modern vision of the Internet of Things.

From 1993 to1997, several companies came out with solutions such as Microsoft's at Work or Novell's NEST. The field gained further momentum when Bill Joy described inter-device communication as a part of his "Six Webs" framework when he presented at the World Economic Forum at Davos in 1999.

Finally, in 1999, The term "Internet of things" itself was coined by Kevin Ashton of Procter & Gamble, later MIT's Auto-ID Center.

1.3 How IoT Works

For the Internet of Things to work as it is, many different technologies had to come together to enable the Internet of Things to be possible. In particular, technologies that allow the various devices and machines to communicate and exchange data are indispensable to the interconnected network that is the Internet of Things.

To begin, before devices can communicate with one another, there is a need for the devices to be able to identify each other as unique entities, and for this, various Identification schemes (IS) and identifiers are used.

The identifiers in an IoT standard can normally be categorised into the following: object identifier, communication identifier, and application identifier. Object identifiers represent physical or virtual objects. For example, Barcodes and Radio Frequency IDentifier (RFID) are some identifiers that cannot be used for the purposes of addressing or communicating. Communication identifiers, on the other hand, identify unique nodes on a network that have communication capabilities. Examples of a network node would be any sensor or network device. The Communication identifier, which is typically made of an IP address, is used for addressing purposes. Finally, Application identifiers identify service layer applications, objects, and logical entities, etc. Some examples of this type of identifier would be Uniform Resource Identifier (URI) and Uniform Resource Locator (URL).

In order to communicate with various IoT applications operating on different IoT platforms and devices, a unified identification methodology is needed. This is the most prominent issue in the IoT, as the interoperability of identifiers is a significant obstacle that needs to be overcome, arising from the fact that many different IoT platforms co-exist. The diverse nature of the hardware devices of different IoT platforms makes it even more challenging for the heterogeneous identifiers to work together. There are many universal ISs in use, including but not limited to: Object IDentifier (OID), Electronic Product Code (EPC), Universally Unique IDentifier (UUID), and International Mobile Equipment Identity (IMEI). These ISs are used in identifying devices and objects in different sectors, such as the supply chain, cellular phones and information systems. Unfortunately, there is no single universally unique IS today, and different platforms use different schemes in the IoT. This makes interoperability across the myriad of platforms a challenge to achieve today.

Another integral part of the Internet of Things is the way devices communicate with each other across the physical distance that separates the objects themselves. In modern times, there are many different technologies that allow this to happen, whether wired or wireless, and across a range of distances that separate these distinct parts of the network.

In the short range, wireless communication between connected devices could be done through various channels, such as: Bluetooth mesh networking, a mesh networking variant to Bluetooth low energy (BLE) with increased number of network nodes, using a standardized application layer; Wi-Fi, a technology used for local area networking operating on the IEEE 802.11 standard, where devices can either communicate through a shared access point or directly between individual devices connected to the network; Light-Fidelity (Li-Fi), a wireless communication technology similar to the Wi-Fi standard, achieving increased bandwidth by using visible light communication; Near-field communication (NFC), communication protocols that allows two electronic devices to communicate with each other within a 4 cm range; Radio-frequency identification

(RFID), a technology that uses electromagnetic fields to read data that are stored in tags embedded in or attached to other items.

For longer ranges, other technologies are more often used, which may be wired or wireless, examples of some would be as follows: 5G wireless networks, which can be used to achieve high communication rates and connect a large number of IoT devices, even while the devices are on the move; Low-power wide-area networking (LPWAN), a type of wireless network designed to allow long-range communication at a low data rate, thereby reducing power and cost needed for transmission; Ethernet, which is a general purpose networking standard that uses twisted pair and fiber optic links together with hubs or switches to allow objects to communicate.

1.4 Consumer Applications of IoT

The Internet of Things can be applied in a large variety of sectors and industries and it is evident in the many IoT devices in use today. Such devices can be broadly classified into consumer, commercial, industrial and infrastructure spaces. In this chapter, we will be taking a look at some of the consumer applications of IoT.

1.4.1 Home Automation

Consumer Internet of Things devices include physical personal devices, such as smartphones, wearables, fashion items and the growing number of smart home appliances, that are now. interconnected via the internet, collecting and sharing data to other devices connected to the network.

As the Internet of things becomes more prevalent, one of the areas where IoT devices are gaining an increasing foothold is in home automation. Examples of IoT devices used in home automation are lighting, heating and air conditioning systems, camera, media and security systems.

There is no denying that adoption of smart home technology is happening at an incredible pace. The Consumer Technology Association (CTA) has estimated around 69 percent of people in the U.S. have at least one smart home device. Outside the US, The International Data Corporation (IDC) reports that the global market for smart home devices grew by 27 percent in 2019 alone, with 833 million devices being shipped that year. Furthermore, the amount of devices shipped is expected to increase to two billion by 2023. In particular, the more popular devices are smart speakers and lights, home monitoring devices, and connected thermostats. Let us take a look at some of their capabilities.

A smart light switch would allow one to switch their lights on and off following a preset schedule, with a digital app, and, with the aid of other devices, respond to voice commands, motion, or even your location.

A smart thermostat has the ability to provide both comfort and cost and energy savings. These devices can establish a heating and cooling schedule based on when one's routine. Furthermore, they can detect when one is home and when they are away, so that their Home ventilation and conditioning system operates only when required, saving energy costs.

All of these devices are usually connected to a home automation system, which typically works by connecting them to a central hub or "gateway". The control of this system can then be manipulated using devices such as wall-mounted terminals, computers, or a mobile phone application which may allow off-site control through the Internet. Smart speakers, such as The Amazon Echo series and Google Home series, are prime examples of such a hub. As these smart speakers have become widely embraced by many other smart home device producers, they have become de facto hubs for their home automation systems, serving as a central point for controlling everything from lights to security cameras and air conditioning systems.

1.4.2 Assistive Functions

Another key application of a smart home is to provide assistance for the elderly and those with disabilities. Home systems can utilise assistive technology to accommodate for an owner's various disabilities. Voice activated commands can assist those with sight impairments or mobility issues while alarm systems can be connected straight to cochlear implants of the hearing-impaired. Safety features such as sensors that detect medical emergencies such as seizures or falls can also be implemented. Smart home technology applied in such a manner can provide users with more personal independence and a higher quality of life.

IoT and AI combined can aid disabled individuals in better reading and understanding the environment around them. This is especially useful for the visually impaired. Take Microsoft's Seeing AI app for example, designed to help visually challenged people learn about their immediate surroundings. The artificial intelligence programmed application can guide walking users away from crowded junctions and even inform the user about the facial expressions of people around them. A similar technology, Cloud Vision API, has also been unveiled by Google for developers to create apps and devices that possess recognition and classification features. The artificial 'sight' of the applications can improve users' understanding and contextualization of physical situations in their surroundings. The ability to better understand their surroundings can help disabled individuals conquer the many communication troubles that they face and can be of much use to individuals with visual, auditory, and cognitive impairments.

IoT technology has also resulted in wearables like smartwatches that can translate content such as emails and texts into Braille or read them aloud to the user. Such devices can improve autonomy of the impaired and help disabled individuals overcome social barriers and mental barriers, thereby allowing them to improve their quality of life with the usage of such accessible smart equipment. Another such innovative developments are smart insoles by Ducere Technologies, an insertable insole that uses vibrations to ease navigation. Other companies are also testing new solutions, such as wearable devices that are reminiscent of radar, and bone-conducting technology to aid in navigation. Such innovations are helpful in overcoming physical obstacles that disabled individuals face, for example, stairs that hinder someone with mobility impairments from entering a building, or curbs that may prevent a disabled individual from using sidewalks.

1.4.3 Wearable Devices

Wearable devices are some of the most prominent consumer lot devices. Wearable devices connect people to the Internet of Things through direct contact with their body: through the wrist with smartwatches and fitness trackers or on a face with smart glasses and virtual reality (VR) headsets.

Wearables have also expanded into the entertainment industry by creating innovative ways to consume digital media. Devices such as virtual reality headsets and augmented reality glasses are forerunners for wearables in entertainment. The influence of these devices no longer remain contained in the gaming industry like the initial days, but are also utilized in the fields of medicine and education.

Virtual reality headsets such as the Oculus Rift, HTC Vive, and Google Daydream View create an immersive media consumption experience by simulating a first-person experience, or by displaying the media and utilizing the user's full field of vision. Similarly, augmented reality glasses are in development by several companies. For example, Snap Inc.'s Spectacles are sunglasses that can record video from the user's point of view and connect to a phone to post videos on Snapchat. Microsoft has also released Augmented Reality glasses, HoloLens, in 2017, exploring using digital holography, to give the user a first-hand experience of Augmented Reality.

Wearable technology has also expanded to include apparel all over the body. Shoes made by the company Shiftwear uses a smartphone application to periodically change the design that is displayed on the shoe, using normal fabric but utilizing a display along the midsection and back of the shoe that displays a design of your choice.

1.4.4 Retail

Retailers are experimenting with implementing IoT into sales models, introducing in-store robots, automation, and drone deliveries into retail stores as these IoT systems can assist and replace menial human tasks. Walmart and Giant Food Stores have implemented robots for cleaning floors and checking inventory.

Another IoT service that may soon be implemented is smart checkouts. Customers will no longer have to interact with cashiers but they can simply pick items off shelves and walk out of the store. Juniper Research estimates that smart checkouts will be powered by AI and computer vision so as to track customers in the store as they pick the items they want. These technologies may lead to annual transactions growth from $42 million in 2019 to an estimated $1 billion by 2023.

Smart delivery and better customer engagement can also enhance customer experience. Domino's, for example, is using autonomous vehicles to deliver food, and other companies such as Amazon and CVS are experimenting with using drones to deliver their goods. Customers are also able to interact with their products before purchase, when buying online, with augmented and virtual reality tools. Gucci, for example, uses AR to allow customers to try on sneakers before purchasing them.

1.5 Commercial Applications of IoT

In the commercial space, IoT devices and technology has been increasingly adopted, and has thus far delivered promising results across a variety of industries.

1.5.1 Healthcare

The Internet of Medical Things (IoMT) is a medical and health related application of the IoT, along with data collection and analysis for research, and monitoring. It is also known as "Smart Healthcare", as the technology is used for creating a digitized healthcare system by connecting available medical resources and healthcare services.

IoT devices could be used to build remote emergency notification and health monitoring systems. These health monitoring devices range from blood pressure and heart rate monitors to advanced devices such as pacemakers, electronic wristbands, or hearing aids. Some hospitals have also begun implementing "smart beds" that senses that they are occupied and when a patient is trying to get up. It can also configure itself to achieve appropriate support to the patient without manual interaction needed from nurses. A 2015 Goldman Sachs report estimates that healthcare IoT devices "can save the United States more than $300 billion in annual healthcare expenditures by increasing revenue and decreasing cost."

Specialized sensors can also be installed in living spaces to monitor the status and general health of the elderly. Such sensors can create a web of smart sensors that can collect, process, transfer, and analyze important information in various environments. Other consumer devices that encourage healthy living, such as connected scales or wearable heart monitors, are available with the IoT.

1.5.2 Industrial Agriculture

Industrial IoT (also known as IIoT) devices receive and analyze data sent from connected equipment, operational technology, locations and people. Together with operational technology monitoring devices, IIoT regulates and monitors industrial systems.

There are numerous ways IoT can be utilized in farming, such as collecting important data on temperature, rainfall level, humidity levels, wind speed and direction, pest infestation, and the soil content. This data can then be used in various ways, such as automating farming techniques, making informed decisions to improve quality and quantity of crop yield, minimising risk and waste, and reducing the amount of effort required to manage crops. For example, farmers can monitor soil temperature, content and moisture remotely, and apply the acquired data to fertilisation programs.

Along a similar vein, Toyota Tsusho started a partnership with Microsoft in 2018 to develop fish farming tools using the Microsoft Azure application suite for IoT technologies regarding water management. Together with researchers from Kindai University, they developed water pump mechanisms using artificial intelligence that could count the number of fish on a conveyor belt, analyze the data, and deduce the effectiveness of water flow from the results of that analysis.

1.5.3 Industrial Manufacturing

The IoT can connect different manufacturing devices equipped with processing, sensing, communication, identification, actuation, and networking capabilities. IoT can be used for smart manufacturing with network control and management of production equipment, situation and asset management, or production process control that IoT brings to the table. IoT intelligent systems hence allow fast production and optimization of new products, and speedy reactions to changing product demands.

Digital control systems that automate process controls, operating tools and service information systems so as to improve plant safety and security can also be achieved with IIoT. IoT can also improve asset management with preventive predictive maintenance, statistical evaluation, and measurements to optimize reliability with the data that it collects from the machines and devices in use.

1.6 Infrastructure

Another application of IoT is the monitoring and operating of urban and rural infrastructures such as bridges, railway tracks and onshore and offshore wind-farms. One such way IoT in infrastructure can be used is for keeping track of any events or changes in structural conditions that could compromise safety and amplify risk.

There are some planned or ongoing large-scale implementations of the IoT, that allows for better management of cities and their systems. Take Songdo, South Korea, for example. The first fully equipped and connected smart city which is currently being constructed, with about 70 percent of its planned business district completed as of June 2018. A large portion of the city is designed to be wired and fully automated, with little to none human intervention required.

Another example would be a current project in Santander, Spain. For this implementation of the IoT, a two-pronged approach is in play. The city of 180,000 citizens have already seen 18,000 installations of its city smartphone app. The app is connected to 10,000 sensors that provide services such as parking space searching, environmental monitoring, and more.

One other large implementation of IoT in a metropolitan scale is the one completed by New York Waterways in New York City, allowing all the city's vessels to be connected and able to be monitored live around the clock in the Hudson River, East River, and Upper New York Bay. With the wireless network in place, NY Waterway is able to take control of its vessels and passengers in a way that was not available previously, improving areas such as security, energy and fleet management and digital signage.

1.7 Criticisms and Controversies towards IoT

While IoT has undoubtedly brought about massive improvements in our quality of life, the technology is still in its infancy. It thus comes with its own set of flaws and criticisms in the gaps that the technology has yet to effectively fill.

1.7.1 Platform Fragmentation

The IoT is plagued with platform fragmentation, lack of interoperability between different systems and common technical standards. This results in a situation where the diversity of IoT devices, whether it is hardware differences, or incompatibility in the software running on the devices, makes the job of developing applications that work consistently between various differing, wildly incompatible systems disproportionally difficult. For example, wireless connections that could be used between IoT devices can be done using Bluetooth, Zigbee, Z-Wave, etc as well as completely custom proprietary radios, each possessing its own pros and cons, as well as unique support ecosystems required to operate them.

1.7.2 Privacy, Autonomy, and Control

Concerns regarding privacy have led many to doubt whether big data infrastructures such as the Internet of things and data mining are in fact incompatible with privacy in its nature. The main challenges of increased digitization in the water, transport and energy sectors are related to privacy and cybersecurity, which requires an adequate response from both researchers and policymakers.

The American Civil Liberties Union (ACLU) has expressed concern regarding the power of the IoT to chip away at people's control over their own lives. The ACLU have stated that "There's simply no way to forecast how these immense powers – disproportionately accumulating in the hands of corporations seeking financial advantage and governments craving ever more control – will be used. Chances are big data and the Internet of things will make it harder for us to control our own lives, as we grow increasingly transparent to powerful corporations and government institutions that are becoming more opaque to us." As IoT usage increases, so will the amount of private information that they will be able to collect from us. Data on our appearance, identity, financial capabilities, living spaces will become more available to devices connected to IoT and may pose a significant risk to our own privacy. Sooner or later, there will be an undeniable need to address such concerns as the IoT rises in its implementation.

1.7.3 Security

Security is one of the biggest threats to the adoption of Internet of things technology. Concerns about the rapid development and implementation that is occurring without appropriate or enough attention paid to the security challenges and the regulatory changes that might be necessary regarding such technology.

Many of the security concerns are similar to those encountered by conventional workstations, servers and phones. Weak authentication processes, not changing default credentials set, unencrypted data sent between devices, and poor handling of security updates are some examples of such concerns. Additionally, many IoT devices do not have much computational power available to be used, resulting in such devices being unable to directly use basic security measures such as installing firewalls or the usage of strong cryptosystems to encrypt data sent between devices; the low prices and consumer focus of many devices makes a strong security system being implemented on the devices even more rare.

IoT devices also have access to massive amounts of data from many different places, and can often control physical devices. It would not be a stretch to say that many Internet-connected appliances such as refrigerators, televisions, and cameras could "spy on people in their own homes". Computer-controlled devices in vehicles such as brakes, engine, locks, and more vital components have been proven to be vulnerable to malicious people who have access to the network. In some cases, vehicle computer systems are connected to the internet, allowing them to be controlled (and therefore manipulated) remotely. Even by as early as 2008 security researchers had demonstrated the capability to remotely control pacemakers without authorization. Later hackers further proved that they could remote control insulin pumps and implantable cardioverter defibrillators.

Poorly secured IoT devices can also be hacked to attack others. In 2016, a distributed denial of service (DDOS) attack enabled by IoT devices infected with the Mirai malware took down a DNS provider and major websites. The Mirai Botnet had infected roughly 65,000 IoT devices in the first day and eventually reached 200,000 to 300,000 infections. These sorts of attacks have cemented the threat and vulnerability of IoT devices in the minds of security experts.

2. Artificial Intelligence

Artificial Intelligence (AI) utilises machines to imitate human thinking and responses. Typically, any form of machinery, including software, that is able to perform actions that are affiliated specially with humans. These actions are not limited to just physical outputs and can vary from simple tasks to complicated projects. Machine Learning and Deep Learning are subsets of AI and thus some sections on AI are further elaborated under these classifications.

Essentially, AI is well sought after for its impeccable learning and processing rates with its ability to cognize information that man cannot. These systems are used very often in our daily lives, being found in player rating systems, transport application systems, stock market predictions and basic operation of companies and organizations.

To surmise, there are 3 different types of AI. Narrow AI, General AI and Super AI.

2.1 Narrow, General, and Super AI

Narrow AI is the most common form of AI that we see in our daily lives. These systems are well programmed to perform very specific functions that we task it to do. Facial and speech recognitions are frequent forms of narrow AI that are utilized. However, narrow AI is only capable of achieving said specific tasks despite its outstanding performance. It is not able to perform actions that are beyond its programmed capacity.

General AI closely imitates human thinking and conduct. It has the ability to consciously think for itself and comprehend different situations in any way that a human would. However, this form of AI has not been attained as machines lack the cognition to apply the same set of knowledge on problems beyond its defined domain.

Super AI is a theoretical AI that surpasses human intelligence and transcends human capabilities. It does not merely understand human actions and bases and instead elicits human behavior such as emotions, inheriting that of a human soul. Super AI's would excel in all that humans are able to do and perform with a higher caliber. Picture a being with its only flaw being that it is too perfect. A being possessing superior physical and mental capabilities that is only limited by its ever-expanding learning rate, beyond our possible imagination. Similar to General AI, this form of AI has not been attained, neither are we close to attaining it. The prospects of Super AI's carries about multiple concerns on how it would affect our civilization and way of life.

2.2 Components and Mechanisms of Artificial Intelligence

Artificial Intelligence is only made possible through a series of components and mechanisms, through which systems are equipped with a semblance of intelligence.

2.2.1 Classifiers and Controllers

The most fundamental programs of AI are classification and controlling. Controllers require classifications before inducing actions.

Classification functions determine classes and groupings through pattern matching. Via supervised learning, predefined data is grouped to their own stated classes and patterns are identified through these groupings, allowing following new inputs and observations to be classified according to these patterns.

Decision trees, artificial neural networks, kernel machines and k-nearest neighbors are widely used approaches for classifiers.

The data that is to be classified significantly governs the performance of classifiers. These characteristics of data include sample size, sample distribution across the different classes and dimensionality. As such, different forms of classifiers need to be used for different forms of data in order to achieve different required outcomes.

2.2.2 Logic

Various categories of logic are used to form parameters and boundaries of AI programs and planning. Some forms for specifications include propositional logic, first-order logic, fuzzy logic, description logic and modal logic. More fundamental forms fall under default logic and non-monotonic logic, these are rudimental senses and help tackle the qualification problem which is the incapability of inputting all the conditions needed for an action to perform properly in actuality. Logics tackling discrepant and conflicting functions include paraconsistent logics. Inductive logic programming is used in Machine Learning too.

2.2.3 Search and Optimization

Search refers to finding a final solution through multiple series of viable solutions. However, a simple full-scale search, in most cases, results in having to sieve through infinite solutions. Resultantly, these searches are inordinately long or end up incomplete. Thus, heuristics are needed to reduce the number of solutions searched to make the task manageable. Optimization is a way of searching where we start off through possible conjectures and continue fine-tuning to a point where further improvements are no longer possible.

2.2.4 Probabilistic Methodologies for Indeterminate Problems

In most cases AI has to run under insufficient and varied information, thus probability methodologies are needed as tools for problem solving. Bayesian networks are used extensively as a generic tool in this aspect. For more complex cases, AI utilizes additional advanced approaches such as the Markov chain Monte Carlo.

Mathematical tools under the concept of utility are also established for planning and decision making. Specific decision tools are also utilized for planning and decision making. Said tools consist of models like Markov decision processes and influence diagrams.

2.2.5 Artificial Neural Networks (ANN)

Neural networks are able to process continual functions and digital logic gates and popular AI culture resulted from utilising neural networks with deep learning. Majority of these networks utilize gradient descent for the topology of their neural networks. ANN may also utilize neuroevolution to generate these topologies too. However, neuroevolution may be better as it is less likely to reach an impasse due to its simplicity.

ANN usually make up deep forward neutral networks, where signal passes happen unidirectionally. These networks include multi-layer perceptrons and radial basis networks. Perceptrons are used with Machine Learning. These networks are essentially deep learning models. ANN also makes up recurrent neural networks (RNN), where temporary dynamic behaviours are allowed.

These networks are utilised through Machine Learning and intelligent control, a form of control for AI computing programmes. The neocortex, which aids in the cognitive functions of real neural networks, is imitated with hierarchical temporal memories. Usually, neural networks are programmed with a backpropagation algorithm, the converse of a set of techniques known as automatic differentiation.

2.2.6 Deep Learning

Deep learning utilizes convolutional neural networks (CNN), a form of ANN, to operate multiple important AI software such as speech and facial recognition, modelling elaborate dynamic systems.

RNNs closely use deep learning programmes to hasten the learning processes in sequential problems. The long short-term memory (LSTM), which is primed by Connectionist Temporal Classification (CTC), is another form of deep learning RNN and is very commonly used.

LSTM with CNNs have profuse complex programme implementations, one being image captioning. In the US, some banks utilize CNN to process written checks and, together with GPUs, are able to visually recognize patterns and sequences.

Google voice used LSTM to function different forms of language processing and modelling. This is now widely available for the general market to use on their mobile devices and has been performing extremely well since it has been released.

2.3 Applications of Artificial Intelligence

AIs are able to do any applicable cognitive tasks that it has been programmed to do. It is a common phenomenon that by the time AI programmes are released for the general market, it is no longer deemed to be AI. This is the AI effect, where many argue that the AI does not have the intellectual capability to think and rather follows what it has been computed to do. However, we need to remember that the simple act of learning, be it supervised or unsupervised, is in essence being able to think and holds the capacity for intellectual outputs.

A popular example for successful AI application is AlphaGo, an AI programme where CNN is paired with Reinforced Learning (RL) and was able to take down international Go champions. Although frowned upon, AI is also able to manufacture Deepfakes, a programme that is able to create falsified media content. This programme is often abused to slander politicians and celebrities of like.

2.3.1 Agriculture

AI has made agriculture more efficient, productive and safe. AI identifies patterns through crop yielding and runs multiple simulations, recognizing the prerequisites needed for highest crop yield etc. It predicts the timelines of crop yielding based on the area's environmental factors. AI also surveys the current environment of crops, making sense of different output numbers to ensure that crops meet required safety standards or its most ideal yielding. AI also uses automation for harvesting and maintenance of crops to maximise productivity in actuality. AI is also used to predict safe genetic modifications that could possibly be done to improve crop standards, contributing to global food security.

2.3.2 Computer Science and Programming

AI has been used very prevalently in computer science for its computing capabilities and most AI engines that have been constructed and released to the general market have gone through the AI effect. Such examples include interactive interpreters and graphical user interfaces. AI has significantly shortened the need for lengthy programming and provides user friendly interfaces that are easily accessible for the general market.

AI can also program other AIs. In an attempt to improve current ANN topology, NASNet, a form of neural architecture search, was created to surpass current systems that are available. NASNet was successful in outdoing present systems available on ImageNet.

2.3.3 Cybersecurity

In a significantly digitized world, cybersecurity is necessary to keep us and our information safe. Corporations and organisations could lose up to billions if affected by hacking attacks including malware. AI and Natural Language Processing (NLP) are used together by security firms by sorting information that is owned into different risk levels, allowing vigilant protection of confidential and critical data that could demolish corporations.

2.3.4 Finance

AI has long been used for fraud detection by banks as ANN programmes are able to highlight irregularities. Banks also use AI for their normal operations, book-keeping, estate management and stock investment as it is readily operational at any hour and reacts aptly to different situations based on its algorithm.

Multiple portfolios in financial firms are fully run by AI systems and have proven to be extremely efficient.

Through algorithmic trading, AIs are able to trade at phenomenal speeds, way beyond human capability. It has the potential to earn over millions independently through high-frequency trading. AIs are able to make well-informed decisions or provide their users with the necessary information to make the right call. It has the ability to use NLP and sieve through different sources online like social media feeds and international news castings and determines the credibility and status of different companies. SQREEM (Sequential Quantum Reduction and Extraction Model) is an AI domain for banks to assimilate and survey the data of clients and recommend suitable wealth management services.

These analyses also aid in financial underwriting by running through credit risk models to determine a client's default probability. Multiple observations and characteristics are utilized in evaluating a client’s credit score and these factors are placed into consideration through the AI system, being very useful for all clientele types, especially those lacking sufficient credit histories.

Auditing of financial statements occurs via the inspection of several different data sets. Auditing risk is reduced through an AI controlled procedure with better credibility whilst taking less time. This increases assurance due to continual audits available with high accuracy and no margins for error.

2.3.5 National Security

AI systems in social security focus more towards regulations and surveillance. Facial recognition systems and NLPs are used concurrently with AI systems for mass surveillance within nations, flagging out potential dangers.

Militants utilise AI heavily for military operations too. AI effectively aids communication, intelligence gathering and cyber operations. Autonomous vehicles and drones rely on AI for many series of activities. Activities could include detecting and confirming potential threats, target acquisition and communication amongst networked automation.

2.3.6 Customer Service

AI in the service sector is frequently found for the replacement of repetitive communication jobs. These systems are also used to better the efficiency of communications, such systems include automated mail processing and automated chatbots.

Automated AI customer services increases the efficiency and quality of customer services as it takes away the need for repeated and common queries of consumers. With programmes such as NLP, customers intonation and language are taken into consideration for apt AI responses. Automated customer service takes the hassle of less important services and enables real customer service representatives to handle complicated cases, significantly increasing work efficiency and quality.

Hotels also utilize AI bots for hospitality services. AI systems are able to predict the needs of guests and reduce repetitive duties of staff. AI has also simplified normal hotel operations by doing routine checks and is able to do extra by offering service bots, virtual assistants and collating guest feedback on hotel standards. This also increases the efficiency and quality of hotel staff to attend to more pressing or important needs of guests.

2.3.7 Marketing and Advertising

AI notates general patterns and activity of consumers online and displays selected goods and services based on these activities. Via the tracking of consumers' digital footprints, advertisements are more effectively placed based on these AI algorithms, letting consumers see what they "want" and "like" to see. These personalized advertisements are very commonly found on social media platforms too, spontaneously offering recommended content for consumers. AI provides these advertisements based on how the consumers respond to certain content, clicking or searching for specific content opens up the opportunity for relevant product placements.

2.3.8 Employment and Recruitment

AI simplifies job hunting with a common platform with user friendly interfaces. The job searching algorithm matches employers and candidates via relevant skill sets and common specifications. These platforms utilize NLP to identify and emphasize certain keywords via programmed algorithms. Software's that grade the quality of resumes are also readily available for potential candidates to increase their chances of getting hired.

AI replaces the need of having a physical recruiter run through mountains of resumes. It is able to screen through resumes and rank candidates after identifying their different qualifications. AI can also estimate the success of candidates based on their portfolios.

2.3.9 Social Challenges

AI can be used to identify social issues that are affecting nations worldwide. AI is used to identify different levels of poverty amongst states via analysis of satellite images that are captured. A United Nations platform, AI for Good Global Summit, utilizes AI for identifying socio-economic problems and various forms of well-researched project planning to tackle these problems. These plans go through multiple series' of testing and predictions before execution.

2.3.10 Transportation

AI is heavily used in our transportation systems in an attempt to reduce margins of error and increase efficiency through automation. Consumers are also able to access AI assisting functions on vehicles such as automatic parking and GPS recommending routes.

Fully autonomous cars are currently under testing stages but are already expected to complete their tasks safely and efficiently. Autonomous vehicles are having a hard time finding their spot due to how complicated transportation systems are but are significantly making progress with the help of more AIs. However, similar to other forms of transportation, these autonomous vehicles will still require users to make decisions in times of danger to maintain the safety of passengers.

In aviation, AI is heavily used during pilot training and has proven to be very effective for simulated flights. Commercial flights are commonly automatic now too and only require pilots during take-off, landing and high-risk situations. NASA utilises AI to perform calculations as these programmes have no room for error performing precise calculations with digits up to multiples of decimal places.

In maritime, AI is used for daily ship operations and maintenance. Situational awareness systems are operated by ANNs and recommended routing systems are currently under testing before operations. AI is able to consistently monitor fleet condition and maximise operating efficiencies. AI has the potential to service the maritime sector extremely well and these systems are still under testing due to the dynamic nature of the maritime sector.

2.4 Challenges

AI undoubtedly has significant impacts on our lives in more ways than one. Changes to the economy by AI directly affect our livelihoods too. Many fear their replacement by AIs as these systems are more productive and efficient. However, to achieve strong computing outputs of AI, supercomputers are needed to achieve breakthroughs. Multitude of programmes and processors are needed to operate complex and hefty tasks and these, unfortunately, do not come cheap. Moreover, even with a higher influx of data, organizations find difficulties utilizing these new and larger forms of data, having more subsequent costs with more upgrades. With this problem of having sufficient costs, many also predict that the evolution of AI will bring about more severe class divides due to the affordability of such novel systems.

AI can only determine outcomes based on the information it is given. Meaning, it cannot discern biases based on information that is given to it. If the information that is used for learning is biased, the AI programmes will cause biases due to this error and thus one must be wary of the learning processes the AI is given to prevent such a problem from occurring.

As mentioned above, the AI effect has also been one of the challenges on recognizing the use of AI in our daily lives. Many have high expectations for AI but there is only so much it is able to do as it is nevertheless limited by the programmes instilled by us humans.

3. Machine Learning

Machine learning is a subfield of computer science that is concerned with building algorithms which rely on a collection of examples of some phenomenon. These examples could come from nature, handcrafted by humans or could also be generated by other forms of algorithms. It is often deemed to be a subset of artificial intelligence. In general, Machine Learning systems are trained with a specific set of data used specifically for training and programming of the system. Afterwards, the system is capable of performing tasks that have not been directly coded to do. This makes Machine Learning broad in its ways of use. The computer programme operates based on its "experiences" towards a certain task and its performance on the task improves with more "experience".

Machine Learning has the main task of making inferences through inductive reasoning. They are to reach probable conclusions with the lack of necessary information, causing uncertainty in their found conclusions. This is essentially what goes on in real life, whereby data that is needed is unavailable or unknown. Thus, formal probability and statistics are utilized to achieve the needed output.

3.1 Parametric Machine Learning Models

A parametric model is a learning model that summarizes data with a set of parameters that are fixed in size. Regardless of the amount of data that is given to the parametric model, the model will not change the number of parameters it needs. The algorithms involve having to select a form for the function followed by learning the coefficients for the function from its given training data.

This holds advantages as this is a fast and simple system that requires very little data. However, its disadvantages hold that strong assumptions have to be made and it is not made to do complicated tasks. There could also be a problem with underfitting of model, this is when the trained model cannot predict targets given in the training set. This occurs as the model needs to be more complex or because the features need to be more informative.

3.2 Non-Parametric Machine Learning

Non-parametric machine learning algorithms are algorithms that do not make strong assumptions about the form of the mapping function. This is extremely useful when there is a lot of data available with a lack of prior knowledge. This reduces the hassle of having to choose the right features for the model.

Its advantages lie in its flexibility of use and high levels of performance. However, a more complex system would definitely need more time and a model with more features would require more data. There may also be issues with overfitting, this is when the model predicts training data well but predicts new test data poorly. Regularization or simpler models have to be used in this case.

3.3 Fundamentals of Machine Learning Algorithms

Some fundamental algorithms utilized by machine learning include systems of linear equations, least squares, linear regression, ridge regression, polynomial regression, optimization, gradient descent, decision trees, random forest.

To ensure the well generalizing (high performance) of the trained algorithm, test sets (with unseen examples) are used to test the prediction of labels of examples. Other important performance considerations are computational speed and efficiency. To attain the most of software quality, the trade-off between computational efficiency and maintainability holds very large factors of consideration.

3.4 Methodologies of Machine Learning

When training machine learning models, there are four primary learning methodologies that are used. These include supervised learning, unsupervised learning, semi-supervised learning, and reinforcement learning.

3.4.1 Supervised Learning

Training data is used with the aim to learn the model's parameters from the given data and labels. These data and labels are all known. During testing, the model uses these learned parameters to predict the label of novel data.

In supervised learning, the dataset is the collection of labelled examples. N refers to the number of samples available. Each element $\mathbf{x}i$, among N is called a feature vector. A feature vector is a vector where each specific dimensions $\mathbf{x}i$ contains values describing the example. This feeds information on the features of the set of data. The label yi can either be an element belonging to a finite set of classes or a real number.

Classification is often used here via a prediction of discrete valued output. Regression is also frequently used via continuous valued output.

3.4.2 Unsupervised Learning

In unsupervised learning, the dataset is a collection of unlabelled examples. Similarly, x is a feature vector, and the goal of an unsupervised learning algorithm is to create a model that takes a feature vector x as input. This input is then either transformed into another vector or a value that can be used to solve a practical problem.

We do not feed the classes to the training model in this case. This allows the machine to sort out the differences in the data through grouping and clustering by discovering the underlying structures of the data. Pictorial summaries are often used to showcase the output of the model.

3.4.3 Semi-supervised Learning

As the name suggests, this form of learning is a mixture of both supervised and unsupervised learning. Both labelled and unlabelled data are inputted for the learning model to proceed. Usually there will be a significantly larger amount of unlabelled data. Classifications that are given from supervised learning pair with the ability to gauge how data distributes through identifying features. Through research it has been found that this form of learning with a small number of labelled data has caused the learning model to be more accurate

3.4.4 Reinforcement Learning

Reinforcement learning involves the machine interacting with the environment through stage changes. A policy is a function that takes the feature vector of a state as input and outputs an optimal action to execute in that state. The action is optimal if it maximizes the expected average reward.

3.5 Data Management

There are many forms of data cleaning for different forms of data to improve the quality of data. These forms of data manipulation are essential for improving the accuracy of models, allowing us to achieve better efficiency and overall performance.

3.5.1 Data Wrangling

Data wrangling is the process of transforming and mapping data from one "raw" data form into (another format to make it more appropriate for downstream analytics. Data wrangling cannot be blindly executed, we must know the need for wrangling.

Examples of data wrangling include scaling to a range, feature clipping, z-score standardization and one-hot encoding.

3.5.2 Data Cleaning

Data cleaning detects corrupt and inaccurate records from a dataset, table or database and either corrects or removes said data. Data cleaning can help effectively deal with missing data and imputation.

3.5.3 Data Integrity

Data integrity maintains the assurance of accurate and consistent data over its entire life-cycle. This is crucial to designing and applying any system that collates, processes or stores data. These are normally in 2 forms of physical and logical integrity.

3.6 Online Applications of Machine Learning

Machine Learning processes have already been extensively adopted and utilized online, where large amounts of data are crunched in order to optimize the output of online processes.

3.6.1 Search Engines

While it may not appear obvious to some, some of the most important features that we take for granted in this day and age online are powered by machine learning. One of the most important uses of this technology could be found in the form of search engines, such as Google, Yahoo or Bing. Search engines are expected to parse the meaning of the millions of searches and bring the most relevant of sources to the forefront of the results page. If the search engine is unable to understand the queries sent its way by the user, it would not be able to begin searching for the appropriate webpages to send the user's way. This is where Machine Learning comes into the picture.

Users are human, and as such, make mistakes when conducting a search query, including errors such as spelling errors and hence search engines cannot assume that users will spell correctly all the time. In fact, many use search engines as a way to find the correct spelling of words they only vaguely remember the letters of. In order for Search Engines to be able to identify the words that users are trying to enter reliably, machine learning is used to be able to identify what users are trying to enter even if they made some kind of spelling mistake.

Furthermore, users will rarely search the exact wordings of the content found in websites, and hence search engines will have to approximate the meanings of the words and their synonyms and work out the most relevant web pages to show in the results. Ambiguous searches would have to be identified by the search engine as well, such as when a user searches "Titanium", the search engine would have to show results pertaining to the chemical element and the song so as to ensure that the user finds the result that they want regardless of which meaning they meant. This too, is machine learning at work.

Another more recent example of machine learning on search engines would be that of Image searching, where users would upload an image, on sites such as Google Image Search, and receive information on the image, and other similar images etc. Machine learning is used here to find the characteristics of the image uploaded and scan through millions of other images in the database and return images with features that are similar, such as composition, colours, subject matter etc.

3.6.2 Advertisements

Another component of the net that makes ample usage of machine learning would be that of advertisements. Modern advertisements allow for better targeting of desired audiences and increased quality and suitability of advertisements shown to potential customers. Being on social media sites such as Facebook and Instagram, or general websites such as Google, advertisements are now better able to target audiences by showing them advertisements that the user may be more inclined to be interested in. Machine learning is used to match users based on their web activity, such as what queries they have entered recently into a search engine, to products that may be relevant to the user's demographics. Machine learning is used to maximise the quality of the user profiling and hence advertisement matching.

3.6.3 Social Media

Another use of Machine Learning is the algorithms that govern the pages of a social media site. Whether it is Twitter's curated Timeline, Instagram's Feed, Tumblr's Dashboard or Youtube's Recommended Videos, many features that users interact with on these sites that bring new and interesting content to the forefront of user attention uses Machine Learning. These sites use data that they know about its users as input and predicts what events, posts or content that its users will be interested in and presents them to the user in hopes of providing a more engaging experience while on these social sites. Without machine learning, modern sites will not be what they are today.

3.7 Financial Applications

One of the more impactful ways Machine Learning is in use today is in the world of Finance and Economics. Machine Learning helps people decide when and where to move money, and has become an indispensable part of the toolset used by those in the sector.

3.7.1 Algorithmic Trading

One way that Machine Learning is used today in the finance sector is in the form of Algorithmic trading. This refers to the use of algorithms to help traders make better decisions when trading with markets. Mathematical models are used by traders to monitor business ners and other trade activities in an attempt to detect factors and signs of change that are about to come that could cause prices of the goods that the trader is trading to rise or fall. The trader would be able to control their trading by entering preset parameters that may arise in a situation so that it would be able to automatically place traders without active input from the trader. Doing so brings about some benefits that a trader may not get if they did the trading themselves without the aid of algorithmic trading. Firstly, algorithmic trading models are able to process and evaluate large volumes of data at any one time to a greater amount of accuracy compared to a single human mind. They are also more nimble on the digital platform, able to process and manage thousands of trades a day, and are able to make fast trading decisions, giving the users an undeniable advantage when using machine learning tools to trade.

Furthermore, algorithmic trading using machine learning does not make any trading decisions based on emotions, unlike its human counterparts that are very often tempted to do so; an affliction that is well known amongst the trade that clouds the judgement of many traders. This trading method, used by the likes of hedge fund managers and financial institutions, allows the trading activities to be automated and free from the fickle minds of emotionally vulnerable humans.

3.7.2 Fraud Detection and Prevention

Another area where Machine learning is used is that of fraud detection and prevention. Fraud is a major problem for financial institutions and causes billions of dollars of losses every year. A large amount of data is kept digitally by finance companies, and the risk of security breaches are significant. With the increasing pace of technological advancement, fraud is now considered a high threat to valuable data.

Fraud detection systems in the past were created with a set of rules in mind, which can now be bypassed by modern fraudsters with relative ease. Hence, most companies today employ machine learning to flag and combat fraudulent transactions by scanning through datasets and detecting abnormal activities and flag them for further investigation. By comparing a transaction against data that they possess, such as account history and IP address, the algorithm can determine if the transaction is potentially abnormal and block the transaction before further review can be taken.

3.7 Data Recognition and Translation Applications

One innovative way machine learning is in use today is in that of Image, handwriting and speech recognition. From automated digitizing of documents, to real time translations and voice to text conversions, the ability for machine learning to take real world data and convert them into digital data is becoming more and more invaluable.

As the world moves on to become more digitised, there is a need for more companies and corporations to transition to keeping records in a virtual space rather than a physical space. However, the process of transitioning is one that is lined with obstacles and errors when one has to manually enter the data into the digital world. In this regard, handwriting and image recognition technology, enabled by machine learning, can dramatically reduce the time taken and mistakes made when transcribing the large amounts of documents into a digital database.

Along a similar vein, image translation, such as the likes of Google Image Translate and Yandex can perform translation services by looking at images of foreign text and translating and overlaying the result on top of the image. This advance in translation technologies reduces the need for an intermediary translator when translating real life texts as users may not be able to manually enter a foreign text when it is written in an unfamiliar script, such as Cyrillic, Chinese, Japanese, Hindi or Arabic for a speaker that is only well versed in the Latin script. Machine learning, in this case, would be what supports the image recognition technology, as well as the translation itself, as it searches its database and provides the closest match to the words to be translated.

A speech translation system, such as Jibbigo, on the other hand, uses speech recognition, machine translation and voice synthesis technologies to translate in real time. A user would be able to say something in their mother language, when it will be taken apart by the application so that the words that are spoken can be determined. A machine translation then occurs and enters the translated words into an algorithm that pulls speech sounds from its database and finally delivers the translated words in the second language with the speech sounds.

3.8 Medical Applications

Another area where there is increasing use of machine learning is in the medical sector. One such application is in the identification of disease and ailment diagnosis, such as in cancer identification and treatment. In 2016, IBM Watson Health unveiled IBM Watson Genomics, a collaboration with Quest Diagnostics which aims to achieve precision medicine by melding cognitive computing and genomic sequencing technologies. Another example would be that of Boston-based biopharma company Berg, which is using machine learning technologies to research and develop diagnostic and therapeutic treatments in areas such as detection and management of prostate cancer.

Similarly, Oxford's P1vital® Predicting Response to Depression Treatment (PReDicT) project is using machine learning and predictive analytics to diagnose patients and provide treatments to them, with an overarching vision of producing a ready-to-purchase emotional test battery to be used in clinics.

There has also been usage of machine learning in the realm of preliminary drug discovery and testing, such as in initial screenings of drug compounds to predict success rates. The MIT Clinical Learning Group is one such user, using machine learning algorithms to aid in their precision medicine research to better understand disease processes for treatment for diseases like Type 2 diabetes.

3.9 Future of Machine Learning

With its immeasurable potential and usefulness in computing and analysing mind bogglingly large amounts of data, machine learning has been and will continue to be used in increasingly large amounts by businesses due to its ability to perform complex tasks much quicker and accurately than human labour ever could. The machine learning market itself is expected to grow from USD 1.03 billion in 2016 to USD 8.81 billion by 2022, a Compound Annual Growth Rate of 44.1%. Big players such as Google, Microsoft, Apple and IBM are already leveraging machine learning capabilities and are spearheading the development of more advanced and complex systems to be used in their business operations. It seems that the presence of machine learning will only be more keenly felt in the future.

4. Conclusion

As our modern world continues on the path towards further digitization and automation, the Internet of Things, Artificial Intelligence and Machine Learning will only become increasingly integrated with every aspect of our lives, from day-to-day living, work and research to developments in various industrial and commercial sectors, be it in production, manufacturing or services. Even as development of our technologies continue at this break-neck speed, we must remain vigilant and make sure that we do not fall victim to tunnel vision; Regulations and security systems must be put in place so as to ensure that our technologies (and with them our invaluable data and information handled by these technologies) do not become easy targets for exploitation for those with malicious intents. The various ethical issues surrounding such advancements that could cause society instability, such as over concerns of privacy or unemployment from the implementation of automated services, will also have to be carefully navigated around and addressed.

With that, it is hoped that this book has provided you with a succinct and effective introduction to the world of IoT, artificial intelligence, and machine learning. Like the legendary Icarus, these cutting-edge technologies may stand to become the wings on which humanity can fly upon to reach heights never before seen, doing feats no one today would have dreamt was even possible.